I didn't know that spiders have fangs

© Aladdin Books Ltd 1997
© U.S. text 1997
Produced by
Aladdin Books Ltd
28 Percy Street
London W1P 0LD

First published in the United States in 1997 by
Copper Beech Books,
an imprint of
The Millbrook Press
2 Old New Milford Road
Brookfield, Connecticut 06804

Concept, editorial, and design by
David West Children's Books

Designer: Robert Perry
Illustrators: Myke Taylor and Jo Moore

Printed in Belgium

Library of Congress Cataloging-in-Publication Data
Llewellyn, Claire.
Spiders have fangs and other amazing facts about arachnids /
Claire Llewellyn ; illustrated by Myke Taylor and Jo Moore.
p. cm. — (I didn't know that—)
Includes index.
Summary: Gives lots of facts about arachnids, especially spiders, such as how
they make webs, hunt, communicate, look after their young,
and defend themselves.
ISBN 0-7613-0599-8 (trade hc). — ISBN 0-7613-0610-2 (lib. bdg.)
1. Arachnida—Juvenile literature. 2. Spiders—Juvenile literature. [1. Arachnids.
2. Spiders.] I. Taylor, Myke. ill. II. Moore, Jo. ill. III. Title IV. Series.
QL452.2.L58 1997   97-1256
595.4—dc21   CIP AC

I didn't know that

spiders

have

fangs

Claire
Llewellyn

COPPER BEECH BOOKS
BROOKFIELD, CONNECTICUT

I didn't know that

Introduction

Did *you* know that some spiders are as big as your face? ... some can live for 28 years? ... scorpions are arachnids too?

Discover for yourself amazing facts about spiders and other arachnids, how they catch their food, what they eat, where they live, and how they defend themselves.

Watch for this symbol that means there is a fun project for you to try.

Is it true or is it false? Watch for this symbol and try to answer the question before reading on for the answer.

I didn't know that

spiders have eight legs. Spiders have four pairs of legs. So do scorpions, harvestmen, mites, and all the other members of the *arachnid* family. This makes arachnids different from *insects*, which have six legs.

Emperor scorpion

SEARCH & FIND

Can you find the insect?

& FIND SEARCH &

Red mite

Wolf spider

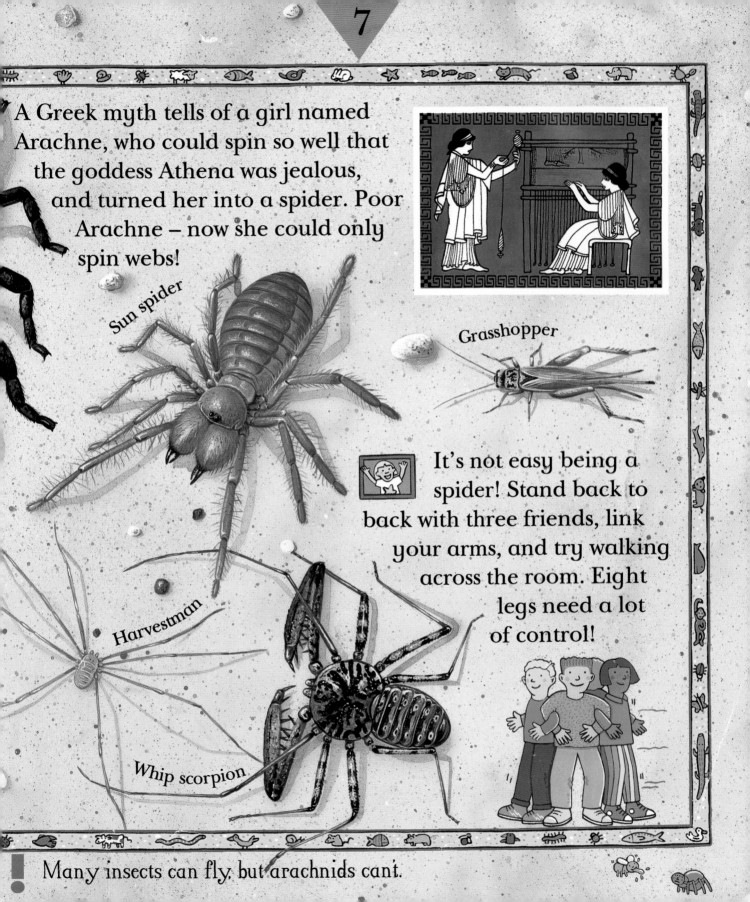

A Greek myth tells of a girl named Arachne, who could spin so well that the goddess Athena was jealous, and turned her into a spider. Poor Arachne – now she could only spin webs!

Sun spider

Grasshopper

It's not easy being a spider! Stand back to back with three friends, link your arms, and try walking across the room. Eight legs need a lot of control!

Harvestman

Whip scorpion

! Many insects can fly, but arachnids can't.

Heart

Liver

Silk glands

Ovary   Book lungs   Intestine

Eyes

Brain

Fang

A spider's body is two halves, joined at the waist. The front has the brain, eyes, jaws, and legs. The back has the heart and *organs* for *digestion*, *reproduction*, and breathing.

The shed skin, or cast, of the tarantula

True or false?
A spider has no bones.

Answer: **True**
Although it has no bones a spider has an *exoskeleton.* This is a hard suit of armor, which protects its body but doesn't grow. As the spider gets bigger, it bursts at the seams and sheds its skin. Underneath, there's a new exoskeleton in a larger size.

I didn't know that

most spiders have eight eyes. These are on the front of their head. In spite of this, many of them can't see very well. They feel their way around with their legs.

Most spiders are soft and easy to eat, but the spiny-backed spider (above) has sharp spines that would stick in a bird's throat.

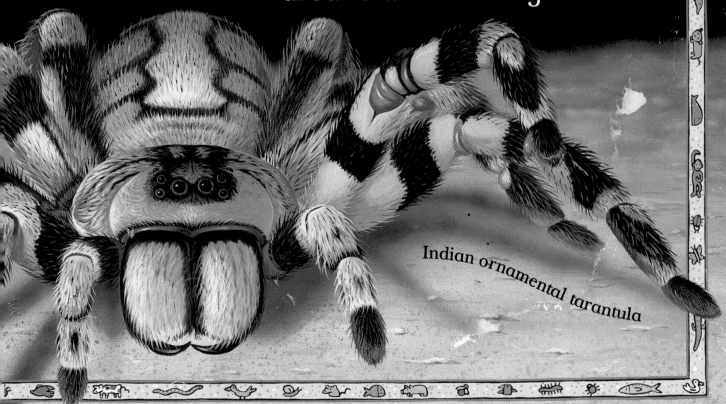

Indian ornamental tarantula

A spider sheds its skin about ten times as it grows.

Silk is made by *glands* inside the spider's body. The silk is runny at first but hardens into a thread when it is pulled out by little tubes called *spinnerets*.

Spinnerets

When an insect gets caught in a web, the spider rushes over, *paralyzes* it with *venom*, and wraps it in sticky silk. Sometimes it saves it to eat later.

Hundreds of years ago, people put spiders' webs on their wounds, believing that this would help stop the bleeding. They were wrong. Putting a web on a wound would just make it dirty.

Orb web spider

The silk in a spider's web could stretch the length of a tennis court.

I didn't know that

spiders make a new web every day. Spiders are always making new webs because their old ones break easily and lose their stickiness. A web traps food for the spider so it is essential for survival and needs to be in perfect order.

SEARCH & FIND • FIND & SEARCH •
Can you find five insects caught in the web?

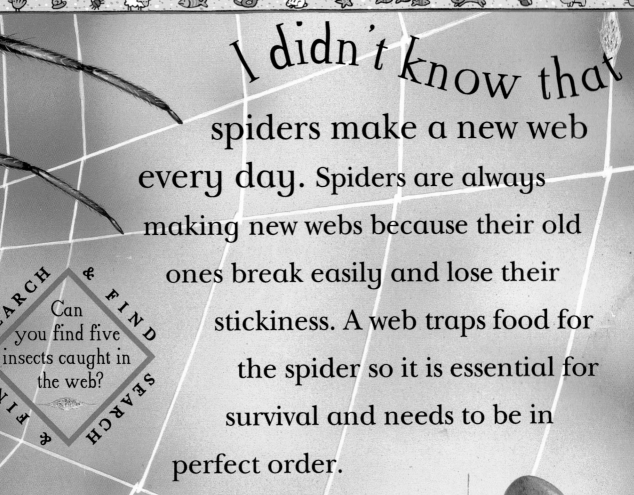

In 1306, King Robert the Bruce of Scotland had been defeated by the English. Hiding in a barn, he watched a spider spinning its web. The spider's hard work inspired Bruce, who returned to the battle and succeeded in beating the English.

Spider silk is stronger than steel wire of the same thickness.

I didn't know that

some spiders live underwater.

Water spiders live in lakes and ponds, but they can't breathe underwater. They spin themselves a bell-shaped web and keep it filled with air by collecting bubbles from the surface.

Turn a glass upside down in a bowl of water. Put one end of a drinking straw under the glass and breathe air into it from the other end. See how the water is pushed out of the glass as the air collects in it. By filling a web with air in this way a water spider has a supply of air to breathe while it is underwater.

Water spider

SEARCH & FIND

Can you find five shrimps?

FIND & SEARCH

The sheet-web spider's web (below) hangs like a trampoline. Above it, the spider spins a series of upright threads. Insects crash into the threads, then fall on the sheet below.

Some spiders lie in wait in their webs, hoping to catch tadpoles.

I didn't know that

some spiders jump through trapdoors. Trapdoor spiders dig a burrow in the ground, cover it with a trapdoor, and hide inside. Then they pounce on any creature that passes.

SEARCH & FIND
FIND & SEARCH

Can you find five ants?

Giant millipede

The bolas spider (left) swings a line of silk with a drop of glue on the end. The glue sticks to the wings of fluttering moths, which are drawn in and devoured.

The net-casting spider (right) spins a net then hangs head down on a thread, holding the net and waiting. When an insect walks by, the spider scoops it up.

The bolas spider is named after the bolas, a South American lasso.

I didn't know that

some spiders spit. Spitting spiders don't use webs. Instead, they make a sticky gum, which they fire out through their *fangs*. This completely covers an insect and sticks it to the spot.

True or false?
Many hunting spiders use safety lines.

Answer: **True**
Like rock climbers, many spiders are attached to a line of silk in case they fall. They can also run up it if they need to escape!

Spitting spider

16

The crafty raft spider hunts small fish and tadpoles by gently tapping on the water with its feet. Fish swim up toward the spider, thinking it must be a tasty fly, and are then grabbed by a pair of jaws.

Jumping spiders stalk their prey slowly like a cat, then suddenly pounce for the kill. These spiders see well with their front pair of eyes, and can measure the distance they need to jump.

Jumping spider

Wolf spiders eat up to 15 insects on a good hunting day.

I didn't know that

spiders have fangs. Like snakes, spiders use poison to defend themselves and kill their prey. A spider jabs its fangs into its victim and holds on while the poison pumps into the prey.

SEARCH & FIND FIND SEARCH

Can you find the lucky bug?

Wandering spider

A spider can't break down food inside its body like we can. Instead, it injects each meal with juices, which change it into soup. Then the spider sucks it all up.

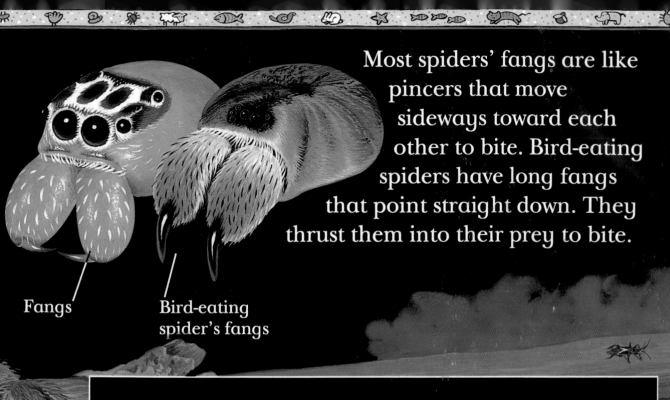

Most spiders' fangs are like pincers that move sideways toward each other to bite. Bird-eating spiders have long fangs that point straight down. They thrust them into their prey to bite.

Fangs

Bird-eating spider's fangs

In Taranto, Italy, 600 years ago, the people suffered from poisonous spider bites. They danced for days, hoping to flush out the poison. The town has given its name to the tarantella dance—and to the tarantula spider!

A spider bite always leaves two little holes in the skin.

A male web spider introduces himself to a female by plucking the threads of her web. He taps out a signal, which brings her running to meet him.

True or false?
A female black widow spider eats her mate.

Answer: **True**
Female black widow spiders are larger and fiercer than the males. After mating, a male needs to make a quick getaway, or the female will eat him up.

Male black widow

Female black widow

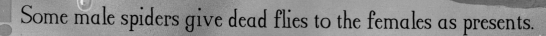

Some male spiders give dead flies to the females as presents.

The barking spider makes a noise by rubbing its mouthparts together.

SEARCH & FIND

The red mark on the black widow spider.

FIND & SEARCH

I didn't know that

some spiders dance when they're courting. Before trying to mate with a female, the male jumping spider dances and prances, waving his colorful legs. The female is dangerous and may need soothing. This dance tells her he's a friend, not a foe.

Male jumping spider

Female jumping spider

21

True or false?
Young spiders can fly.

Answer: **False**
Young spiders can't fly, but they sometimes sail through the air on a line of silk. This is known as *ballooning*. Ballooning can be risky, but it is a good way for spiders to spread out from the nest.

Scorpions (above) make very good mothers. They carry their young on their back, and try to protect them from danger.

Wolf spider

Most spiders lay their eggs in a parcel of silk and hide it away somewhere safe. But the wolf spider carries her parcel around with her until the eggs are ready to hatch.

22

Nursery-web spider

I didn't know that spiders have nurseries. Just before her eggs hatch, the nursery-web spider spins a tent of silk. It's a nursery, where the tiny baby spiders stay safe and sound, while their mother keeps guard nearby.

SEARCH & FIND
Can you find 10 balloonists?
FIND & SEARCH

After they have hatched, baby spiders still need a parent's protection.

I didn't know that

some spiders can change color. Crab spiders are masters of disguise and can match their color to their surroundings. This clever trick keeps them hidden inside flowers, where other spiders would be more easily seen.

SEARCH & FIND & FIND SEARCH &

Can you find ten crab spiders?

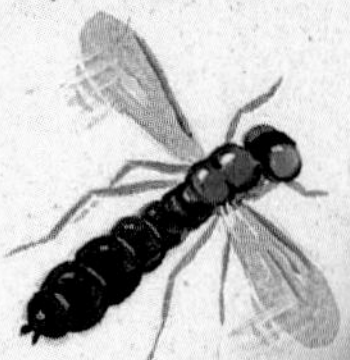

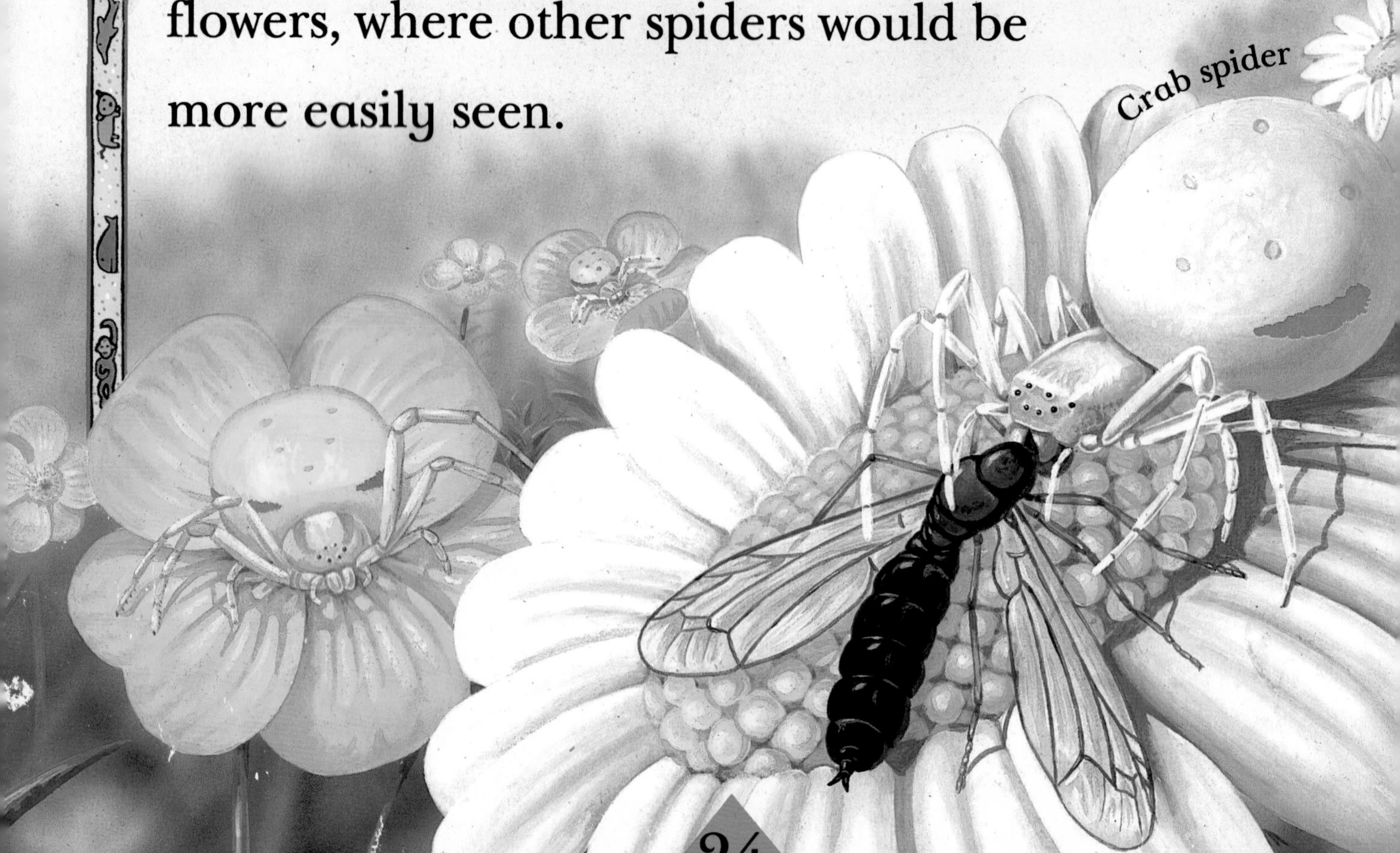

Crab spider

24

When they are threatened, some tarantulas (right) brush tiny, hooked hairs off the back of their body. When the sharp hairs land on an animal's skin, they make it feel itchy and sore.

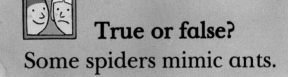 **True or false?**
Some spiders mimic ants.

Answer: **True**
Some spiders look just like ants, except that they have two extra legs! This can be a useful disguise because ants sting, so many creatures leave them alone.

Ant-mimic spider

I didn't know that

wasps attack spiders. The female tarantula hawk wasp feeds her babies tarantulas. She attacks, stings, and paralyzes these huge spiders, then drags them into a hole and lays an egg on them.

Tarantula hawk wasp

SEARCH & FIND
Can you find five wasps?
FIND & SEARCH

Cactus wren

Collared lizard

Desert tarantula

Spiders are soft and tasty, and have many enemies, such as *mammals*, birds, lizards, ants, beetles, scorpions – and even other spiders!

Many farmers kill pests by spraying their crops with chemicals. The sprays kill spiders, too. This is a shame because spiders eat many pests, and are really the farmer's friend.

A golden-wheeling spider escapes by cartwheeling down sand dunes.

I didn't know that

some spiders are bigger than this page. The world's biggest spider is the Goliath bird-eating spider, which grows up to 11 inches wide. The world's smallest spider, the Patu marplesi, is so small that you could fit ten of them on the end of your pencil.

Patu marplesi

The most charming, intelligent spider is Charlotte in the book *Charlotte's Web* by E. B. White. Charlotte lives in a barn, and saves the life of Wilbur, her good friend the pig.

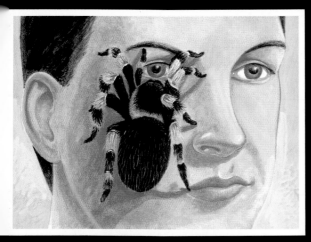

People who are scared of spiders suffer from a fear known as arachnophobia. They should avoid the horror film *Arachnophobia* (above) – it's definitely not one for them!

Goliath bird-eating spider

One of the world's most poisonous spiders is the funnel-web spider from Australia. Its venom is deadly to some animals, such as *primates* and creepy crawlies. But to many other mammals, like cats and dogs, it's harmless!

Glossary

Arachnid
An animal, such as the spider, that has eight legs.

Ballooning
The way in which spiders spread out, by flying through the air on a line of silk.

Camouflage
The colors and markings on an animal that help it to blend in with its surroundings and make it difficult to see.

Digestion
The body's system of breaking down food and changing it into a form that the body can use for nutrition.

Exo-skeleton
The hard outer covering that protects the body of spiders and many other animals.

Fang
The long, clawlike part of a spider's body that injects poison.

Gland
A part of the spider's body that produces a special chemical substance, such as poison or silk.

Insect
A creature with six legs and three parts to its body.

Mammal

An animal, such as a cat, that gives birth to live young and feeds its babies on milk.

Organ

Any part of the body that has a special purpose. The stomach is the organ for digestion.

Paralyze

To hurt an animal's body so that its muscles can no longer work. Spiders paralyze their prey by injecting them with poison.

Primates

A group of mammals that includes monkeys, apes, and humans.

Reproduction

The way in which animals produce their young.

Spinneret

One of several small tubes on the back of a spider that squirts out the silk used for making webs.

Venom

The poisonous liquid that spiders inject into their prey when they bite.

Index